FREEDOM'S
PROMISE

IDA WELLS
JOURNALIST AND ACTIVIST

BY DUCHESS HARRIS, JD, PHD
WITH SAMANTHA S. BELL

Core Library
An Imprint of Abdo Publishing
abdobooks.com

Cover image: Ida Wells wrote about violence against
African Americans in the late 1800s and early 1900s.

THIS BOOK CONTAINS
RECYCLED MATERIALS

Cover Photo: Sallie E. Garrity/National Portrait Gallery, Smithsonian Institution
Interior Photos: Sallie E. Garrity/National Portrait Gallery, Smithsonian Institution, 1; Chicago
History Museum/Archive Photos/Getty Images, 5, 43; North Wind Picture Archives, 6–7; Marion
Post Wolcott/Farm Security Administration/Circa Images/Newscom, 10; Everett Historical/
Shutterstock Images, 12; Horace Bradley/Bettman/Getty Images, 16–17; Circa Images/Newscom,
20, 22; Bettman/Getty Images, 24–25, 30; Jonathan Ernst/Reuters/Newscom, 27; Red Line Editorial,
29, 40; Charles Rex Arbogast/AP Images, 34–35

Editor: Maddie Spalding
Series Designer: Claire Vanden Branden

Library of Congress Control Number: 2018966064

Publisher's Cataloging-in-Publication Data

Names: Harris, Duchess, author | Bell, Samantha S., author.
 Title: Ida Wells: journalist and activist / by Duchess Harris and Samantha S. Bell
  Other title: Journalist and activist
  Description: Minneapolis, Minnesota: Abdo Publishing, 2020 | Series: Freedom's promise |
      Includes online resources and index.
   Identifiers: ISBN 9781532118760 (lib. bdg.) | ISBN 9781532172946 (ebook)
    Subjects: LCSH: Wells-Barnett, Ida B., 1862-1931--Juvenile literature. | African American
          women journalists--Biography--Juvenile literature. | African American educators--
          Biography--Juvenile literature. | African American women civil rights workers--
          Biography--Juvenile literature.
     Classification: DDC 323.092 [B]--dc23

CONTENTS

A LETTER FROM DUCHESS

In the late 1800s and early 1900s, mobs of white people killed thousands of African Americans in the United States. These killings were called lynchings. Mobs lynched Black people for minor or perceived insults. Often the victims had not committed a crime. But they did not receive a fair trial. White people used lynchings to control and oppress Black people. Black journalist Ida Wells was one of the first to investigate lynchings. She researched and documented more than 700 lynchings. Her work helped expose widespread violence against African Americans.

Wells's work and legacy continue to be recognized today. In 2018 the city of Chicago, Illinois, renamed a street after Wells. It is now called Ida B. Wells Drive. Wells lived in Chicago for much of her life. Michelle Duster is Wells's great-granddaughter. She was proud to learn that Wells will be recognized in this way.

Please join me in this exploration of Wells's life and legacy. Follow me on a journey that tells the story of the promise of freedom.

Duchess Harris

Ida Wells brought attention to injustices against African Americans through her writings.

SEPARATE AND NOT EQUAL

In May 1884, 21-year-old Ida Wells stepped aboard a train in Memphis, Tennessee. Wells was an African American woman. She had purchased a first-class ticket. She made her way to the only first-class car. She sat down and pulled out a book to read. When the conductor of the train came through, he saw Wells sitting there. Other African American passengers were riding in the second-class smoking car. That car was reserved for smokers and African Americans. The conductor demanded that Wells move to the smoking car too.

In the mid- to late 1800s, black people could work as servers in railroad cars but could not sit with white passengers.

The smoking car was crowded and dirty. It was filled with cigarette smoke. Besides, Wells had paid for a seat in the first-class car. She refused to move. The conductor grabbed her arm, but Wells bit his hand. He called two other men to help drag her out. Still, Wells refused to move to the other car. She got off at the next stop instead.

LIMITED FREEDOMS

Because of the color of her skin, Wells was not allowed to sit in the first-class train car. This experience was common among African Americans in the South at the time. White people discriminated against black people in many ways.

After the American Civil War (1861–1865), African Americans enjoyed some new rights and opportunities. The Thirteenth Amendment was passed in 1865. This amendment abolished slavery. But many white people tried to restrict black people's rights. In 1865 and 1866, southern leaders created laws called the black codes.

These laws were designed to control black people. Black men could be arrested for talking to white women. They could also be arrested or forced to pay a fine for being unemployed. Black people who were unable to pay the fine could be forced to work for no wages.

In 1877 a new group of white people came into power in the South. These lawmakers believed that white people were better than people of other races. They created Jim Crow laws. These laws built on

PERSPECTIVES
SEGREGATION ON TRAINS

In 1884 Wells sued the railroad company that made her leave the first-class car. A Memphis jury ruled in her favor. The court ordered the railroad company to give her $500. The ruling also said that railroad companies had to provide first-class cars for black passengers. The railroad company took the case to the Tennessee Supreme Court. The court disagreed with the jury. It said that the railroad's second-class smoking car for black people was equal to the first-class car for white people. The court forced Wells to pay $200 in fines.

Some restaurants had separate entrances for black people.

the black codes. They also enforced racial segregation. Racial segregation is the separation of people into groups based on race. White and black people were separated in public spaces. Black people had to use separate services and facilities. These services and facilities were often worse than those provided to white people. African Americans were treated as second-class citizens.

MURDER, NOT JUSTICE

In the late 1800s, mob violence was out of control in the United States. Mobs of white people threatened, injured, or killed black people they perceived as a threat. Often the mobs accused their victims of committing a crime. There did not have to be proof that the person had committed the crime. A rumor was enough. This type of murder was called a lynching. Many white people who lynched black people belonged to the Ku Klux Klan (KKK). The KKK was a hate group with many members across the country. White southerners formed the KKK in 1866.

Lynch mobs tried to justify their actions. They said they were lynching criminals. But there was no trial, judge, or jury. Many of the people who were lynched did not do anything wrong. Some white people lynched black men for getting too close to white women. White people also targeted successful black people. Some black people had started their own businesses. Some were trying to exercise their rights as US citizens,

such as the right to vote. The Fifteenth Amendment gave black men the right to vote in 1870. Many white people did not want black people to have this right. They did not think black people should be treated as citizens. They used lynchings to control and intimidate black people.

When a crime was committed against a white person, innocent black people were often blamed. As US citizens, African Americans had the right to a fair trial. But they were often denied their legal rights.

Lynching even became a social event. Newspapers advertised lynchings. Often a crowd of spectators watched. Sometimes they traveled long distances to get to the location. Railroads ran special trains to get people there. Sometimes people dressed up and brought along picnic baskets. Photographers took pictures of the lynchings. Men, women, and children

By the 1920s, the KKK had more than 1 million members.

LYNCH LAW

The term *lynching* can be traced back to the Revolutionary War (1775–1783). Colonel Charles Lynch was a judge from Virginia. He supported the American colonists in their fight against the British. In 1780 he ordered men who supported Britain to be tied to a tree and whipped. This type of punishment without fair trial became known as "lynch law." In the 1800s, the meaning of the term changed somewhat. Lynching came to mean torture and murder. White people used lynching as a way to control black people, especially in the South. By the 1880s, 90 percent of lynchings in the United States took place in the South.

watched and cheered as the accused people were tortured and murdered.

White communities and law enforcement allowed lynching to continue for many years. Wells wanted more people to be aware of this injustice. She decided to take action. She began investigating lynchings. She wrote newspaper articles and gave speeches against lynching. She was determined to stop this violence.

STRAIGHT TO THE
SOURCE

In 1900 Wells gave a speech to an audience in Chicago, Illinois. In her speech, she explained that lynching had become widespread:

> Our country's national crime is lynching. It is not the creature of an hour, the sudden outburst of uncontrolled fury, or the unspeakable brutality of an insane mob. It represents the cool, calculating deliberation of intelligent people who openly avow that there is an "unwritten law" that justifies them in putting human beings to death without complaint under oath, without trial by jury, without opportunity to make defense, and without right of appeal. . . .
>
> Lynchings began in the south, rapidly spreading into the various states until the national law was nullified and the reign of the "unwritten law" was supreme.

Source: Ida B. Wells. "Unwritten Law." *Lapham's Quarterly*. Lapham's Quarterly, 1900. Web. Accessed November 15, 2018.

What's the Big Idea?

Take a close look at this passage. How did Wells describe lynching? How did she describe the people who committed lynchings?

CHILDHOOD AND EARLY CAREER

Ida Wells was born on July 16, 1862. Her family was enslaved on a plantation in Holly Springs, Mississippi. The United States was in the midst of the Civil War. Many white people in the Confederacy wanted to protect and expand slavery. Mississippi and ten other southern states were part of the Confederacy. Northern states made up the Union. Many people in the Union wanted to stop the spread of slavery. Some wanted slavery to be abolished.

In the 1800s, enslaved people in the South were forced to do hard labor, such as picking cotton.

Ida was the oldest of eight children. Ida's parents taught Ida and her siblings the importance of getting an education. After the war ended, Ida's family was free. Her father worked for Shaw University in Holly Springs. Shaw provided education to newly freed slaves. Ida's father was part of a group that made important decisions for the school.

Ida received her early education at Shaw. Her parents told her to learn all that she could. While she was there, she discovered how much she loved reading. She read

PERSPECTIVES
A. C. MCDONALD

A. C. McDonald founded Shaw University. He was a white man who wanted to give former slaves and their children a good education. Many of the teachers at the university shared this goal. Most were white women from the North. In 1875 McDonald described the purpose of the school. He said it was to "lay well a foundation for a broad, thorough and practical education, such as shall fit our pupils for long lives of usefulness to themselves, their race, and the church." In 1890 Shaw University was renamed Rust College.

every book in the school's library. But she realized that she had never read a book written by or about African Americans.

LOSS AND CHANGE

When she was 16 years old, Ida went to visit her grandmother in the countryside in Mississippi. While Ida was there, an outbreak of a deadly disease called yellow fever spread through Holly Springs. Many people died, including Ida's parents and her baby brother. Ida wanted to keep her family together. With the help of relatives and friends, she took care of her brothers and sisters. Ida needed a job to earn money for the family. She took a teaching exam and passed. She became a teacher at a one-room schoolhouse. The school was about 6 miles (10 km) from Holly Springs. She attended classes at Shaw during her summer breaks.

In about 1882, Ida's situation changed again. Her brothers left home to find jobs. Ida and her sisters moved to Memphis to live with their aunt. Ida took

Many black students were enrolled at Fisk University in the late 1800s and early 1900s.

another teaching exam so she could teach children in Memphis schools. She took classes at Fisk University in Nashville, Tennessee.

BECOMING A WRITER

In the late 1800s, segregation affected the jobs that were available to black people. Many employers would not hire black people. Some African Americans started their own businesses. These businesses included newspapers. African Americans started hundreds of newspapers across the country. Many white newspapers did not explore the stories and perspectives of black people. Those that did often covered black people's stories in racist ways. African Americans wanted to speak out against discrimination. Black-owned newspapers allowed black people to share

THE AMERICAN NEGRO PRESS

In 1919 the American Negro Press (ANP) was founded. Today, the term *negro* is widely considered offensive. But in the early to mid-1900s, this term was commonly used to refer to African Americans. The ANP was the largest black news agency in the United States. ANP reporters gathered and wrote news stories. The agency distributed these stories to black newspapers across the country. From these stories, black readers could learn about what was going on in other black communities. ANP writers were all African Americans. The ANP gave black people a way to freely express their views.

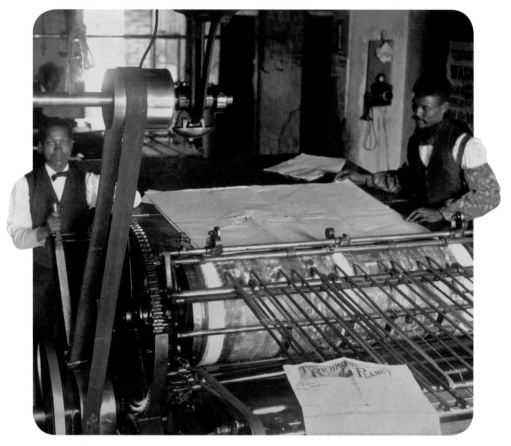

Many black people started their own newspapers in the late 1800s and early 1900s to have their voices heard.

news and ideas. These newspapers connected African American communities.

In 1887 Ida began writing for a church newspaper in Memphis. She wrote about racial and political issues in the South. Her first article was about the incident on the train. Her articles soon appeared in other church newspapers. Many people praised her work. Her career as a writer had begun.

A few years later, Ida became an editor and a part owner of the *Free Speech and Headlight*. This was a black newspaper in Memphis. She wrote articles about the terrible conditions in the city's black schools. Conditions in white schools were often much better than those in black schools. Ida criticized the Memphis school board. The school board was in charge of running the city's schools. In response, the school board refused to renew Ida's teaching contract. She lost her teaching job. But now she had more time to write.

EXPLORE ONLINE

Chapter Two covers Ida's childhood, education, and early career. The article at the website below goes into more depth on these topics. Compare the information on this website with the information provided in Chapter Two. What information is the same? What new information did you learn from the website?

IDA B. WELLS
abdocorelibrary.com/ida-wells

SPEAKING OUT

I n 1892 Wells received horrible news. A mob of white people had lynched her close friend, Thomas Moss. The mob had shot and killed him.

Moss had co-owned a grocery store. It was called the People's Grocery. It was located in a mostly black neighborhood near Memphis. A white man named William Barrett owned a grocery store in the same neighborhood. The People's Grocery was successful. Barrett did not like this competition. He wanted to close the People's Grocery.

On March 2, 1892, a black boy and a white boy got into a fight near the

Demonstrators wear nooses around their necks to protest lynching in 1934.

People's Grocery. The incident soon got out of hand. Groups of white and black people joined the fight. Barrett was attacked near the People's Grocery. He claimed that Will Stewart, a black clerk who worked at the People's Grocery, had attacked him.

On March 3, an attack happened in a different grocery store in the neighborhood. A white grocery store clerk shot a black man.

This incident frightened black residents. Barrett fed into their fear. He knew that officers would soon arrive at the

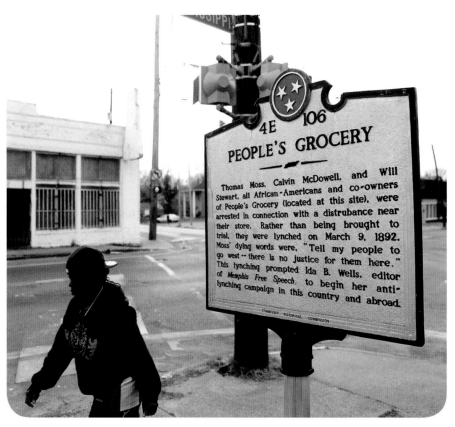

A sign on a street corner in Memphis marks the site of the 1892 People's Grocery lynching.

People's Grocery. They would arrest any black people they thought had been involved in the fight the night before. Barrett started a rumor that a white mob was coming to destroy the People's Grocery. Moss and other workers at the store knew that the police would not protect them. They put armed guards around the store.

At night, a sheriff and five other armed officers marched toward the People's Grocery. The guards thought the officers were the white mob. They fired at the men. They wounded some of the men. The police responded by arresting more than 100 black people in the neighborhood on the morning after the shootout. Moss was arrested. Moss and most of the people who were arrested had not been involved in the incident. Moss was not one of the guards. He had not committed any crime. He had just been in the store when the incident happened. Stewart and another black worker, Calvin McDowell, had also been in the store. The police took Moss, Stewart, and McDowell to a local jail.

On March 9, a group of 75 white men entered the jail in the middle of the night. They kidnapped the three men. Moss begged for his life for the sake of his family. But the mob shot and killed the men.

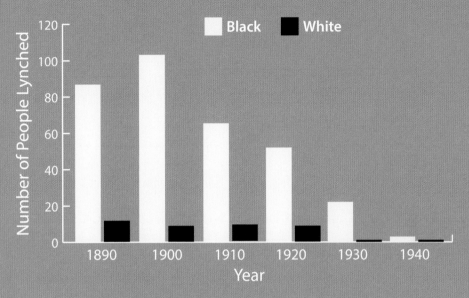

LYNCHINGS IN THE UNITED STATES

The above graph shows the number of black and white people lynched in certain years in the United States. What can you tell about lynching by looking at this graph?

A NEW CAUSE

Grieving and angry, Wells started an anti-lynching campaign. She began investigating lynchings in the United States. She traveled throughout the South to places where lynchings had occurred. Wells documented more than 700 lynchings. She interviewed witnesses. She studied photographs

Lynchings continued to occur in the United States through the mid-1900s. Young Emmett Till was lynched in 1955 for allegedly flirting with a white woman.

and local newspaper articles. She published her findings in the *Free Speech and Headlight*. Soon other newspapers reprinted her articles.

Wells's articles outraged many white people. While she was traveling, she learned that people had broken into the *Free Speech and Headlight* office. They destroyed furniture and left a note. In the note, they threatened to kill anyone who tried to publish the newspaper again. Wells also learned from friends in Memphis that white men were spying on her home. They threatened to kill Wells. To escape these threats, Wells decided not to return to Memphis. She moved to New York.

ACTIVISM

Wells continued her activism in New York. She began writing for a newspaper called the *New York Age*. She gave public speeches and continued to investigate lynchings. She found that white people often killed African Americans for minor or perceived insults. These insults included not paying a debt or disrespecting a white person. In 1892 Wells published a pamphlet called *Southern Horrors: Lynch Law in All Its Phases*. A pamphlet is a small book with information on a certain subject. In Wells's pamphlet, she noted that lynchings had increased as African Americans became more educated and successful. White people used lynchings to oppress and terrorize black people.

WOMEN'S CIVIC CLUBS

While in England, Wells learned about women's civic clubs. These clubs helped women become involved in politics. Ida took this idea back to the United States. She encouraged women to join civic clubs. She helped start the National Association of Colored Women's Clubs (NACWC) in 1896. The NACWC is a civil rights organization. In its early years, it advocated for women's suffrage, or the right to vote. At the time, women did not have voting rights.

In 1893 Wells traveled to England, Scotland, and Wales. She met with leaders and gave speeches. People packed churches and lecture halls to hear her speak. She spread the word about violence against African Americans. She gained support from people in other countries. She believed they could pressure Americans to address the problem of lynching. Wells helped establish the London Anti-Lynching Committee in London, England. Her work inspired activists to create similar groups in the United States.

STRAIGHT TO THE
SOURCE

Frederick Douglass was an African American writer and antislavery activist. In 1892 he wrote a letter to Wells. He praised her pamphlet *Southern Horrors: Lynch Law in All Its Phases*:

> Let me give you thanks for your faithful paper on the lynch abomination now generally practiced against colored people in the south. . . .
>
> Brave woman! you have done your people and mine a service which can neither be weighed nor measured. If American conscience were only half alive . . . if American moral sensibility were not hardened by persistent infliction of outrage and crime against colored people, a scream of horror, shame and indignation would rise to Heaven wherever your pamphlet shall be read.

Source: Ida B. Wells. "Southern Horrors: Lynch Law in All Its Phases." *Project Gutenberg*. Project Gutenberg, February 8, 2005. Web. Accessed January 14, 2019.

Consider Your Audience
Adapt this passage for a different audience, such as your friends. Write a blog post conveying this same information for the new audience. How does your post differ from the original text and why?

MAKING A DIFFERENCE

I n 1893 Wells met Ferdinand L. Barnett in Chicago, Illinois. Barnett was an African American lawyer. He was also an editor and an activist. He owned Chicago's first African American newspaper.

In 1894 Wells moved to Chicago. She married Barnett the following year. Members of women's civic groups attended the wedding. They supported Wells's work and activism. Her supporters filled the church and the streets outside the church. The wedding was announced in both African American and white newspapers.

Michelle Duster, great-granddaughter of Ida Wells, holds a portrait of Wells in 2011.

STILL GOING STRONG

Wells bought Barnett's newspaper, the *Chicago Conservator*. She became the newspaper's editor. After her first child was born, she continued to write and speak out about women's rights. She took her baby with her when she traveled. This was unusual at the time. In the late 1800s and early 1900s, most women stopped working after they married or had children.

After her second child was born, Wells gave up the newspaper. She later had two more children.

She planned to give up public work for awhile to raise her children. She believed being a mother was a job in itself. But she sometimes got called back into public activism. In 1898 she met with President William McKinley. She spoke with McKinley about a lynching that occurred in South Carolina. She returned to work as a full-time activist after her youngest child was old enough to attend school.

In 1909 Wells helped found the National Association for the Advancement of Colored People (NAACP). The NAACP is a civil rights group. It brings attention to discrimination and injustices against African Americans. Wells worked with other NAACP members. They asked for more educational and employment opportunities for African Americans. They also advocated for civil rights, including voting rights. Black men had been granted the right to vote in 1870. But white people tried to stop them from voting. Southern lawmakers created restrictions that kept black men from voting. These restrictions included literacy tests and fines.

WOMEN'S SUFFRAGE

Wells faced discrimination as both a woman and an African American. She wanted both African Americans and women to have political power. She believed that gaining voting rights would be an important step toward equality. In 1913 Wells cofounded the Alpha Suffrage Club. It was the largest black women's suffrage club in Illinois. The club helped black women learn how to become active in government and politics.

Women's suffrage groups marched in parades to bring attention to their cause. Wells planned to march in a suffrage parade in Washington, DC, in 1913. The organizers made black women march at the back of the parade. But Wells wanted to march with other women from Illinois. She left the back of the parade and joined two white women who supported her views.

The women's suffrage movement wanted all women to have voting rights. But white suffragists often excluded and ignored black women. Wells wanted to fight against this racism within the movement.

WELLS'S LEGACY

In 1920 the Nineteenth Amendment was adopted. It gave all women the right to vote. Wells helped women register to vote. She encouraged black women to participate in politics. Wells was also an activist within her community. She was concerned about the high rates of poverty and crime in Chicago's black neighborhoods. Politicians were not addressing these issues. Wells decided to run for the Illinois state senate.

THE NEGRO FELLOWSHIP LEAGUE

In 1910 Wells founded the Negro Fellowship League (NFL). It was located in a Chicago neighborhood that had a high rate of crime and poverty. The NFL's mission was to help black men who were uneducated, poor, and unemployed. The NFL sheltered men who were homeless. It helped men find jobs. It also helped defend men who had been unjustly imprisoned or accused of crimes.

MAP OF WOMEN'S SUFFRAGE

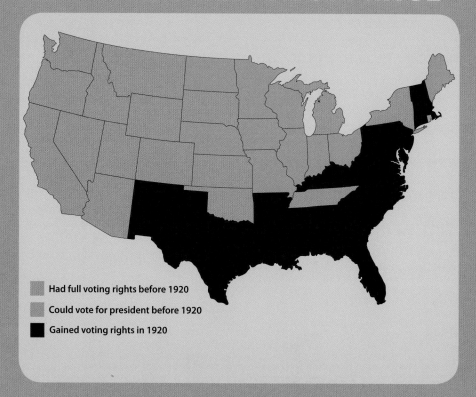

Had full voting rights before 1920

Could vote for president before 1920

Gained voting rights in 1920

Before the Nineteenth Amendment was passed in 1920, some states gave women the right to vote. The above map shows the states where women could vote before this amendment. Alaska and Hawaii are not included. They did not become states until 1959. What do you notice about where these states are located? Why do you think these states were more open to women's suffrage?

She did not win. But her campaign was historic. She was one of the first black women to run for political office in the United States.

Wells died on March 25, 1931. But her legacy lives on. Some of the organizations she cofounded, such as the NAACP, are still around today. She worked hard as a writer and an activist to fight racial discrimination and violence. She exposed the horrors of lynching. She inspired hundreds of women to get involved in politics. She wanted all Americans to truly be free.

FURTHER EVIDENCE

Chapter Four covers Wells's contributions to the civil rights and women's suffrage movements. What was one of the main points of this chapter? What evidence is included to support this point? Read the article at the website below. Does the information on the website support this point? Does it present new evidence?

JIM CROW STORIES: IDA B. WELLS
abdocorelibrary.com/ida-wells

FAST FACTS

- Ida Wells was born into slavery in Mississippi in 1862.

- Wells started her education at Shaw University in North Carolina.

- Wells's parents and young brother died from yellow fever. Wells and her sisters later moved to Memphis, Tennessee. In Memphis, Wells worked as a teacher and a journalist.

- Wells wrote articles about racial inequality. In 1892 Thomas Moss, one of Wells's close friends, was lynched. Wells began an anti-lynching campaign in response.

- Wells investigated lynchings throughout the South and published her findings. She traveled to Europe to speak out against lynching.

- Wells cofounded civil rights groups such as the NAACP. She also joined the women's suffrage movement.

- Wells ran for the Illinois state senate. She lost the race but inspired other black people to run for office. She helped women become involved in politics.

STOP AND
THINK

Tell the Tale

Chapter One of this book talks about the time when Wells was forced out of a first-class train car. Imagine you were traveling in the same car. Write a journal entry describing what you saw and how you reacted.

Surprise Me

Chapter Four discusses some of Wells's work for the civil rights and women's suffrage movements. After reading the chapter, what facts about her work did you find most surprising? Why? Write a few sentences about each fact.

Take a Stand

Wells brought attention to violence and injustices against African Americans. What injustices are still committed against African Americans today? Do you think Wells's speeches and work are still relevant?

GLOSSARY

abolish
to officially end or do away with something

amendment
a change or an addition to an existing law

colonist
someone who lives in a colony, or a land owned by a faraway nation

discrimination
the unjust treatment of a person or group based on race or other perceived differences

jury
a group of people at a trial that decides whether a person accused of a crime is guilty or not

plantation
a large farm where workers grow crops

poverty
the condition of being poor

segregation
the separation of people of different races or ethnic groups through separate schools and other public spaces

sue
to file a lawsuit, or a case, against a person or group in court

suffragist
someone who supports people's voting rights

ONLINE
RESOURCES

To learn more about Ida Wells, visit our free resource websites below.

Visit **abdocorelibrary.com** or scan this QR code for free Common Core resources for teachers and students, including vetted activities, multimedia, and booklinks, for deeper subject comprehension.

Visit **abdobooklinks.com** or scan this QR code for free additional online weblinks for further learning. These links are routinely monitored and updated to provide the most current information available.

LEARN
MORE

Bailey, Diane. *Ida B. Wells*. New York: Aladdin Books, 2019.

Harris, Duchess, JD, PhD. *Women's Suffrage*. Minneapolis, MN: Abdo Publishing, 2018.

ABOUT THE
AUTHORS

Duchess Harris, JD, PhD

Dr. Harris is a professor of American Studies at Macalester College and curator of the Duchess Harris Collection of ABDO books. She is also the coauthor of the titles in the collection, which features popular selections such as *Hidden Human Computers: The Black Women of NASA* and series including News Literacy and Being Female in America.

Before working with ABDO, Dr. Harris authored several other books on the topics of race, culture, and American history. She served as an associate editor for *Litigation News*, the American Bar Association Section of Litigation's quarterly flagship publication, and was the first editor in chief of *Law Raza*, an interactive online journal covering race and the law, published at William Mitchell College of Law. She has earned a PhD in American Studies from the University of Minnesota and a JD from William Mitchell College of Law.

Samantha S. Bell

Samantha S. Bell lives with her family in upstate South Carolina. She graduated from Furman University with a degree in history and teaching certification in social studies. She is the author of more than 90 nonfiction books for children.

INDEX